AF604609

WOMEN
IN
GREAT
AUSSIE
SPORTS
AUSSIE
RULES
TONY LA TORRACA
REDBACK
publishing

First Published 2023 by
Redback Publishing
PO Box 357 Frenchs Forest NSW 2086
Australia

www.redbackpublishing.com.au
orders@redbackpublishing.com.au

ISBN 978-1-76140-026-1 HBK

Author: Tony La Torraca
Editor: Caroline Thomas
Designer: Redback Publishing

Original illustrations © Redback Publishing 2023
Originated by Redback Publishing

Acknowledgements
Abbreviations: l—left, r—right, b—bottom, t—top, c—centre, m—middle
We would like to thank the following for permission to reproduce photographs: (Images © shutterstock, Getty Images)

COVER IMAGE Tayla Harris by DustNail via Wikimedia Commons, p4t Sydney FC vs Perth Glory 2019 W-League Grand Final 2019GF - Kennedy (48781198026).jpg by 2019GF - Kennedy via Wikimedia Commons, 4b Tayla Harris kick 23.03.19.jpg by DustyNail via Wikimedia Commons, 5m Katie Brennan 23.02.20 by DustyNail via Wikimedia Commons, 6b First AFLW Ball Up 03.02.17.jpg by Tigerman2612, via Wikimedia Commons, p7t Lauren Pearce 03.02.18 by DustyNail via Wikimedia Commons, p8t Bec Goddard.jpg by Flickerd via Wikimedia Commons, p8b Alan McConnell.jpg by Flickerd via Wikimedia Commons, p9m Belindas.png by KateorMe via Wikimedia Commons, p11b Angela Foley kicking.5.jpg by Flickerd via Wikimedia Commons, p12 Lauren O'Shea and Tara Morgan ruck contest.2.jpg by Flickerd via Wikimedia Commons, p13t Eleni Glouftsis 2019.1.jpg by Flickerd via Wikimedia Commons, p13b Aishling Sheridan 28.02.20.jpg by DustyNail via Wikimedia Commons, p14t shutterstock_3453421/max blain, p14b AFLW Umpires in 2019.jpg by Allied45 via Wikimedia Commons, p15 AFLW at North Sydney Oval.jpg by Avatar5991 via Wikimedia Commons, 17t Fremantle AFLW team.jpg by Flickerd via Wikimedia Commons, 19m Carlton Anthem 03.02.17.jpg by DustyNail via Wikipedia Commons, p20t Daisy Pearce 18.02.17.jpg by Tigerman2612, via Wikimedia Commons, 20b Daisy_Pearce_interview_Tom_Harley.jpg by Flickerd via Wikimedia Commons, 21t Tayla Harris by Kelly Defina / Stringer/ GETTY IMAGES, p21b Tayla Harris kicking 3 23.03.19.jpg by DustyNail via Wikipedia Commons, p22t Skilled-stadium-geelong.jpg by Marcus Wong via Wikipedia Commons, 22t Ellie_Blackburn_04.02.18.jpg by DustyNail via Wikipedia Commons, p22b Nikki Gore 2019.3.jpg by Flickerd via Wikipedia Commons, p23t Ash Riddell 27.03.21 (cropped).jpg by DustyNail via Wikipedia Commons, p23b Georgie_Prespakis_2022.jpg by Storm machine via Wikipedia Commons, p24 Ankit Mvia Shutterstock, p24t Madison_Prespakis_2019.2, by Flickered via Wikipedia Commons, p24b Kiara_Bowers_2019.4, by Flickered via Wikipedia Commons, p25t Erin_Phillips_kicks_19.03.17_(cropped) by DustyNail via Wikipedia Commons, p25b Brianna_Davey_(2)_04.03.17 by Tigerman2612 via Wikipedia Commons, p26 AFLW Coaches 2022 by Dylan Burns/ AFL Photos / Stringer / GETTY IMAGES, p28t Phillips, Erin, Alberton Oval 2022 September 3.jpg by Thejoebloggsblog via Wikipedia Commons, p28m Emma_Kearney_27.03.21, by DustyNail via Wikipedia Commons, p28b Kiara_Bowers_2019.1, by Flickered, via Wikipedia Commons, p29t Madison_Prespakis_23.03.19_(cropped) by DustyNail via Wikipedia Commons, p29m Bri_Davey_28.02.20_(cropped) by DustyNail via Wikipedia Commons, p29b Emily Bates 19.03.17.jpg by Tigerman2612 via Wikimedia Commons.

A catalogue record for this book is available from the National Library of Australia

CONTENTS

The AFLW Game 4
Women's Draft 6
Player Positions 7
Coaching 8
Training 9
AFLW-specific Rules 10
General AFL Rules 12
The Umpires 14
The Field of Play 16
The Beginnings of the Women's Football League 18
Player Profiles 20
The AFLW Teams 26
The MVP Award 28
Premiership Winners 30
Glossary 31
Index 32

THE AFLW GAME

AFLW is Australia's women's national semi-professional Australian rules football league.

Most Attended

The AFLW is the most attended women's football competition in Australia with a record attendance of 53,034 in the 2019 Grand Final. This was the highest attendance of any women's club championship anywhere in the world.

The Adelaide Crows won their third AFL Women's premiership, defeating the Melbourne Demons by 13 points in the 2022 AFL Women's Grand Final, at Adelaide Oval.

Television Coverage

In its inaugural 2017 season, all AFLW matches were televised live. As part of the broadcast deal, two free-to-air television networks covered the costs of broadcasting one Saturday-night game per week, plus the league's opening match and Grand Final. The Premiership season matches were covered by a pay-TV network.

Tayla Harris

A Great Spectacle!

In Australian rules football, each team moves the ball over the playing field to score goals. The speedy movement of the ball, the overhead marking, the fierce tackling and the accuracy of the kicking makes for a great spectacle.

Salary

The salary of AFLW players is four times more than any other professional women's team sport in Australia and it is still rising! The pay scale is split into four tiers depending on individual players' results.

Exciting Skills

Aussie rules is a game of skill, strength and athleticism. One of the most exciting skills of the game is high marking. This means kicking the ball high and long.

Katie Brennan is an Australian rules footballer and captain of the Richmond Football Club in the AFLW competition

Establishment

In 2010, the AFL commissioned a report into the state of women's football around the country. This report recommended the establishment of a national women's league. New stand-alone clubs were considered before deciding to use the resources and branding of the existing men's AFL clubs.

WOMEN'S DRAFT

The first women's draft was held on 15 May 2013. This determined the playing lists for the exhibition match on 29 June 2013. It was the first time that two women's sides had competed under the banners of AFL clubs.

Exhibition Matches

The success of these exhibition matches demanded the formation of a nationwide women's competition that began formally in 2017. This was a bold move, considering that the league had previously announced plans to simply 'consider' a women's competition 'sometime before 2020'. The already-planned 2016 exhibition series was expanded and a total of ten matches were played across Australia.

The first ball up in the Carlton v Collingwood game of the inaugural AFLW Premiership

Inaugural Teams

The inaugural teams were announced on 8 June 2016 with the Adelaide Crows being crowned as the league's first premiers. They defeated the Brisbane Lions in the Grand Final held on Saturday, 25 March 2017. The first season of the league had eight teams. This had expanded to 10 teams by the 2019 season, 14 teams by 2020 and to 18 teams in 2023. In 2022, 14 teams played 10 rounds and three weeks of finals. There was also a Pride Round and an Indigenous Round.

The Team

Each AFLW team has 16 players on the field and five players on the bench. Games are played in summer and players can get hot and thirsty. Five players wait on the bench to change places with those on the field and can do this as many times as necessary during the game, to ensure no player becomes dehydrated or exhausted in the heat.

PLAYER POSITIONS

The Ruck

Rucks follow the ball. They are known as followers.

The Back Line

The back line can be the two back pockets and the full-back, or both the full- and half-back lines which form the complete defence.

The Centre Line

Centre line players recover balls from the back line as well as set up scoring shots.

The Half-back Line

Half-backs recover the ball from the back line and clear the ball forwards.

Lauren Pearce is an Australian rules footballer She plays for the Melbourne Football Club in the AFLW competition

The Forward Line

Full-forwards attack the goal and trap the ball in that area.

The Half-forward Line

Half-forwards set up scoring shots, attack the goal and try to trap the ball in that area.

COACHING

In 2019, the AFL partnered with sponsors to launch the Women's Coaching Crusade. This forged a commitment to grow the AFLW with more female coaches, partnership awards and scholarships that fully fund the 'Next Coach' program.

New Coaches

New and prospective coaches can attend the annual AFL Coaches Study Tour and receive mentorship from experienced AFL Coaches.

AFL Women's Coaches

Since the AFLW was inaugurated in 2016, much work has gone into the recruitment and training of new female coaches, as none had previously existed at a professional level. All AFLW teams had male coaches until three women stepped into the roles. Bec Goddard took over for the Adelaide Crows from 2017 to 2018, Michelle Cowan took over for the Fremantle Dockers from 2017 to 2018 and Peta Searle took over St Kilda from 2020 to 2021. By 2022, a further 26 female coaches had graduated from the BHP Women's Coaching Academy and there is now a steady stream of new recruits.

Bec Goddard was the AFLW's inaugural premiership coach, leading the Adelaide Crows to the 2017 premiership.

Alan McConnell

Alan McConnell has coached AFL for more than 30 years. He now works for the NSW Institute of Sport in Coach Development. His role is to lead the training of new and developing coaches as part of a national strategy to promote excellence in sport.

TRAINING

AFLW is a game of running, kicking and leaping for marks. Successful players must have great skill, but athleticism is just as important. AFLW players tone and train their bodies to build upper-body strength without bulking on too much muscle weight.

Science

Science has taken over in creating fit players. Modern training devices, fitness experts, dietitians, specialised coaches and all the equipment of the gym are used to keep players in top condition.

Belinda Smith is an Australian rules footballer. She plays for the West Coast Eagles in the AFLW competition

The Mind Game

Mental health is a very important part of a sportsperson's personal fitness. It is important to develop positive ways to deal with the high expectations of fans, coaches, family members and even yourself. A strong and healthy body needs a strong and healthy mind in charge.

Match Day

The day of the game starts with light jogging before the team is taken through a matchday program by the fitness staff. The program is designed to warm-up the players, without straining them.

After the Game

A few hours after the match, players start their recovery program. Their muscles and skeleton are strained during a game and must be kept toned without applying any further strain. Swimming laps in a pool is great recovery exercise. The player follows up the swim with light gym work.

AFLW-SPECIFIC RULES

Ball Size

AFLW uses a size four ball. It is a little smaller than the size five ball that is used in the AFL competition. Analysis has shown the slightly smaller ball is easier for women to mark.

The special edition, Pink Sherrin had silver reflective writing. It was a throwback to the first AFLX season

SUITABLE FOR GRASS SURFACES ONLY

SHERRI

AFL

KANGAROO BRAND ®

The Stand Rule

The stand rule was first used in the women's competition in 2022. Once the umpire has called "Stand", the player must not move sideways on their line. They are allowed to jump on the spot until the umpire calls "play on".

Boundary Throw-ins

Boundary throw-ins are used to restart play after the ball has gone out of bounds. They are made 10 metres inside the boundary line, with the hope that they land about 25 metres into the field of play. This creates more space for players on either side of the contest and reduces secondary stoppages.

Last Disposal Between the Arcs

If the ball goes out of bounds between the forward and defensive 50 arcs as a result of a kick or handball, the opposing team will receive a free kick where the ball crossed the line. If it is not clear who touched the ball last, it is thrown in. This rule reduces congestion and secondary stoppages.

Centre Bounce 5-6-5

Similar to the AFL's 6-6-6 rule, AFLW has an altered rule because they have 16 instead of 18 players. At centre bounces (or ball-ups), each team must have five forwards and five defenders inside their 50 metre arcs. Three midfielders plus the ruck should be in the middle of the ground and a winger should be on the long side of the centre square.

Bounce

There is no traditional bounce in AFLW. Instead, the umpires throw up the smaller ball in the centre or around the ground.

GENERAL AFL RULES

There are two main aims in AFL rules: to give players fair possession of the ball and to have as few game flow hold-ups as possible.

Ruck Contests – Prior Opportunity

Since 2019, rucks have been allowed to take possession when contesting a ball-up or boundary throw-in. This is no longer seen as having 'prior opportunity'.

Lauren O'Shea and Tara Morgan in a ruck contest

AFLW Scoring

Players score either with a goal which is six points, or a behind, which is one point. Goals are scored by kicking the ball through the goal posts at your scoring end. The ball should not touch the post or be touched by another player, but it can touch the ground. If the ball hits the behind post, then the ball is out-of-bounds. If it was touched or hit the ground first, then it is a throw-in. If it hits the behind post on the full, a free kick is awarded to the defensive team.

A behind is awarded if:

– the ball hits the goal post or goes between the goal post and the behind post
– a goal is scored with a hand instead of a foot, or
– the ball goes through the goal posts after touching a player on the ground.

Eleni Glouftsis

Penalties in AFLW

When a player breaks a rule, a free-kick can be awarded by a centre umpire. Rule breaks can include incorrect disposals, head-high tackles, pushing a player in the back while they have the ball, illegal holds, or a ball going out-of-bounds on the full from a kick. Players must dispose of the ball quickly and legally to stop a tackler being rewarded with a free-kick.

Kick-ins

After a behind, a player will kick-in from the mark, 15 metres away from the top of the goal square.

New Rules for 2023

– If a player kicks a goal from outside the 50 metre arc, nine points are awarded instead of six.
– Umpires will call "play on" instead of awarding a mark for players kicking backwards to team-mates.
– Defenders can kick out from a behind straight away, instead of waiting for the umpire to wave the flag.
– Once the umpire has called "stand", the player on the mark cannot move sideways on their line – jumping on the spot is allowed until the umpire calls "play on".

Aishling Sheridan is an Irish sportswoman who plays Australian rules football for the Collingwood Football Club in the AFLW competition

THE UMPIRES

There are four different types of umpires and one type of steward in a typical game of Australian rules football. At the professional level of AFL there are four boundary umpires.

Goal Umpire

Goal umpires are responsible for all disputes at the goal-line, such as whether or not a ball has scored a goal, a behind, or even failed to cross the goal-line. Goal umpires are the official score-keepers. A goal umpire signals a score at their end of the ground by raising their index fingers in front of them at waist height, using one finger for a behind and two for a goal. Both goal umpires at opposite ends of the field then wave flags to confirm and record the score.

AFLW umpires

Ignoring the Umpires

If a player does not follow the instructions of the umpires, a 50 metres penalty can be awarded as well as the free-kick brought 50 metres closer to the goal.

A record crowd at the North Sydney Oval with 8,264 spectators

Field Umpire

The field umpire, also known as a central umpire, is responsible for controlling general game play. They are the only type of umpire who can award free kicks or call stoppages. They also throw the ball-ups to restart play.

Boundary Umpire

The boundary umpire is responsible for deciding if the ball has left the field of play and whether it left on the bounce or on the full. They are responsible for throwing the ball back into play when it has left the field of play (a throw-in) and for assisting the goal umpire if there is a set shot for goal, by watching the ball from the behind post.

THE FIELD OF PLAY

AFLW is played on a field that is roughly oval in shape. The dimensions of the field vary between 110 and 135 meters in width, and 135 and 185 meters in length.

Player Positions

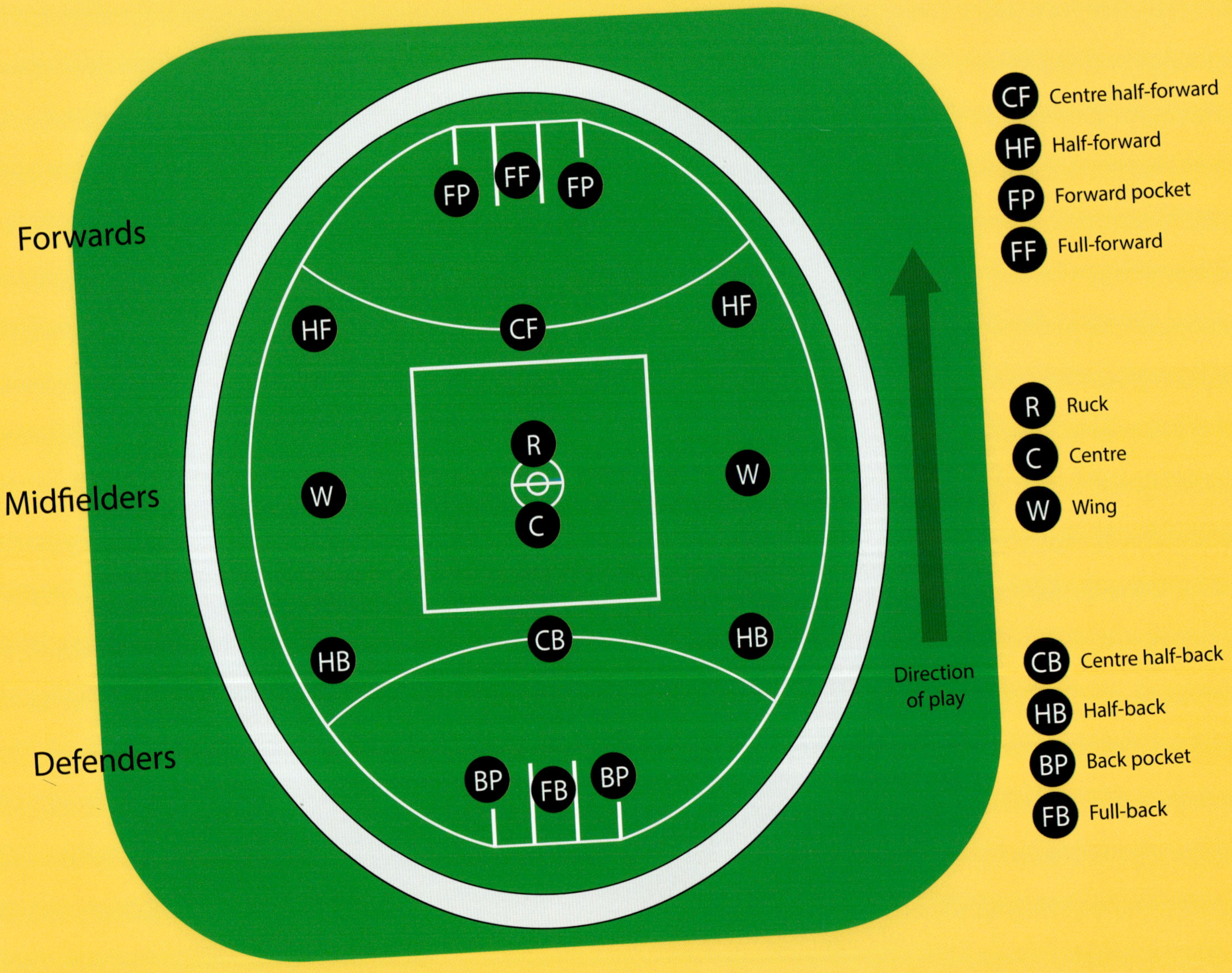

Forwards

FP FF FP

HF CF HF

Midfielders

R

W C W

HB CB HB

Defenders

BP FB BP

Direction of play

- CF Centre half-forward
- HF Half-forward
- FP Forward pocket
- FF Full-forward

- R Ruck
- C Centre
- W Wing

- CB Centre half-back
- HB Half-back
- BP Back pocket
- FB Full-back

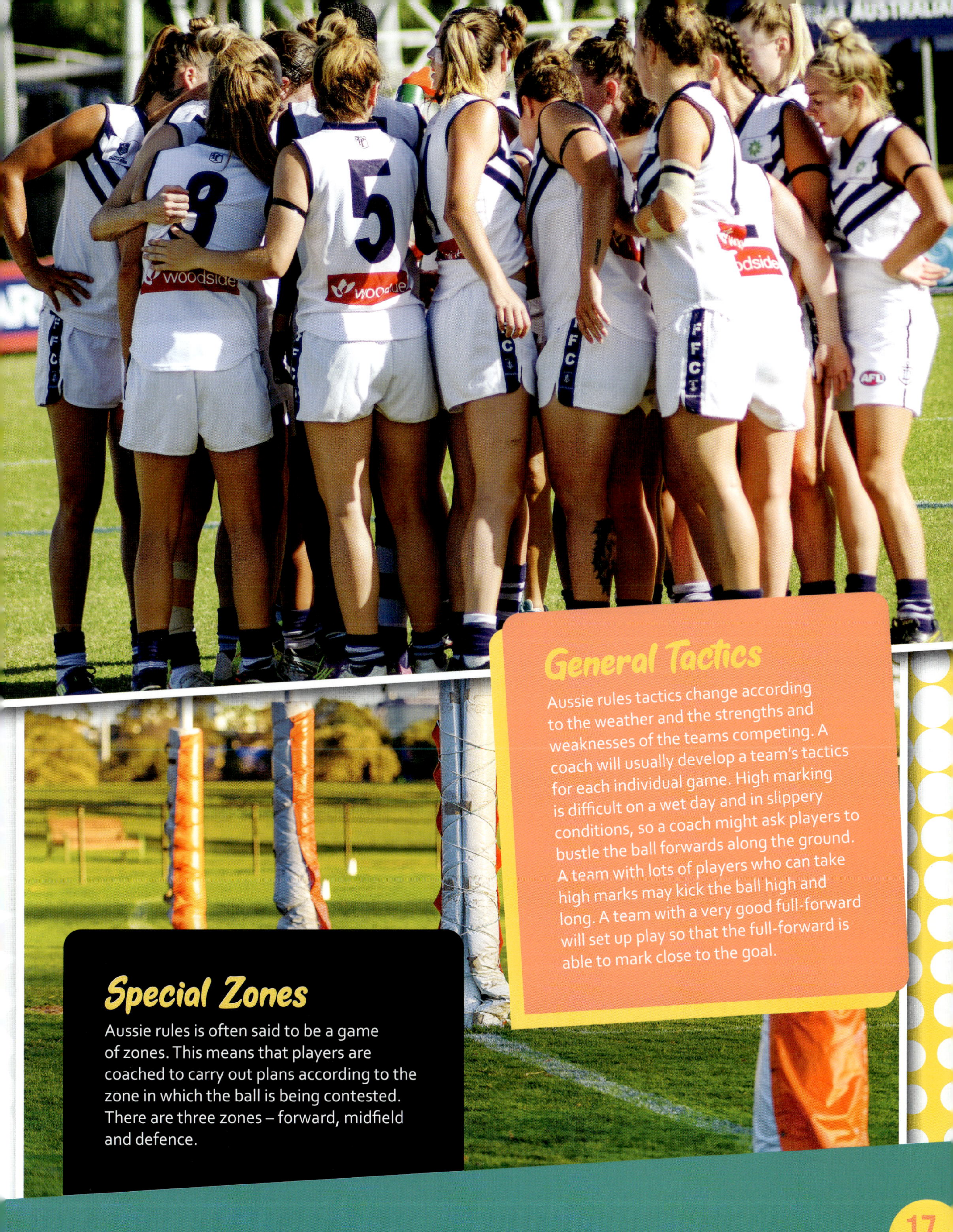

General Tactics

Aussie rules tactics change according to the weather and the strengths and weaknesses of the teams competing. A coach will usually develop a team's tactics for each individual game. High marking is difficult on a wet day and in slippery conditions, so a coach might ask players to bustle the ball forwards along the ground. A team with lots of players who can take high marks may kick the ball high and long. A team with a very good full-forward will set up play so that the full-forward is able to mark close to the goal.

Special Zones

Aussie rules is often said to be a game of zones. This means that players are coached to carry out plans according to the zone in which the ball is being contested. There are three zones – forward, midfield and defence.

THE BEGINNINGS OF THE WOMEN'S FOOTBALL LEAGUE

Since the creation of Australian rules football in the mid-19th century, women have been playing the game and taking part in their own local competitions. It took over 150 years to develop a professional female league.

In 1894, Nellie Stewart, Florence Maude Young and other female celebrities played in a charity football match at the East Melbourne Cricket Ground

Early Amateurs

From the early 20th century, AFL clubs hosted occasional female round-robin tournaments and exhibition matches. Meanwhile, female players developed their own local and regional amateur competitions.

Taking the First Steps

Instead of creating separate female clubs it was decided that existing AFL clubs should have the opportunity to develop a second professional team. Of the 18 AFL clubs, 13 put in bids for AFLW licences. The inaugural season eventually included eight teams.

Distribution

The league distributed the teams according to existing patterns of support across the country. Four teams represented Victoria, with one each for New South Wales, Western Australia, South Australia and Queensland.

Opening Match

The first match of the new competition was played on 3 February 2017 between the Collingwood Magpies and the Carlton Blues. It was planned as a free event at the Olympic Park Oval in Melbourne, the home ground for Collingwood and hoped to attract a crowd of between 5,000 and 10,000 people.

Venue Change

After a series of unadvertised practice matches attracted huge crowds, the AFL had to move the venue to Ikon Park stadium, the Carlton Blues' home ground which was much larger.

The Carlton side line up

The Atmosphere

The atmosphere was described as hot, noisy and electric. People had been pouring into the stadium since the late afternoon, and emotions were high. There was much excitement and many people shed tears at the spectacle of history being made.

Record-breaking Crowds

More than 24,500 people attended the opening match and people had to sit in the aisles or on fences, while thousands more waited outside the gates. It was the largest crowd that season and a record for any women-only sporting event that had ever been played in Australia – excluding the Olympic or Commonwealth Games.

PLAYER PROFILES

There have been many great players in Women's AFL who have changed the game and made themselves heroes. Like many others, Daisy Pearce and Tayla Harris have made huge contributions to the game and deserve special mention.

Melbourne Football Club Homeground

Daisy Pearce

Daisy Pearce captained the Melbourne Demons Football Club from the competition's inaugural season until her retirement in 2023, as well as during its previous exhibition games. Pearce is a dual AFL Women's All-Australian and a three-time AFLW Players' best captain, having won the award in her first three completed AFLW seasons. In 2023, she became a development coach for the men's AFL game at Geelong Football Club.

Director

Pearce is the first woman to be elected as a director on the board of the AFL Players Association. She has a successful media career as a commentator, is an ambassador for the sport and an AFL talent coordinator.

Tayla Harris

Tayla Harris was one of two marquee player signings announced by Brisbane in anticipation of the league's inaugural 2017 season. She made her league debut in the club's inaugural match, in round 1, 2017, against Melbourne at Casey Fields. In round 2, she was nominated for the league Rising Star award for a two-goal, twelve disposal and seven-mark performance against the Fremantle Dockers and was named "Player of the Week" by the AFL Players Association. At the conclusion of two rounds, she was ranked equal fourth in the league for total goals scored (two) and first in the league for contested marks (eight). At the end of the season, Harris was listed in the 2017 All-Australian team.

Immortal

Tayla Harris has been immortalised in a bronze statue that stands in Federation Square in Melbourne. Her iconic high kick is now famous.

Ellie Blackburn

Ellie Blackburn became the Western Bulldogs co-captain in 2019, and has been the sole captain since the 2020 season. Blackburn is the Western Bulldogs games record holder with 58 games, is a three-time AFLW All-Australian (2017, 2018, 2021) and three-time Club Champion

Nikki Gore

Nikki Gore was selected for the 2018 SANFLW Team of the Year and won South Adelaide's best and fairest award. She represented South Australia at the 2018 AFL Women's Under 18 Championships and was selected for the initial squad of the All-Australian team. In 2019, Gore averaged 18 disposals over seven games, laying 48 tackles during the SANFLW season.

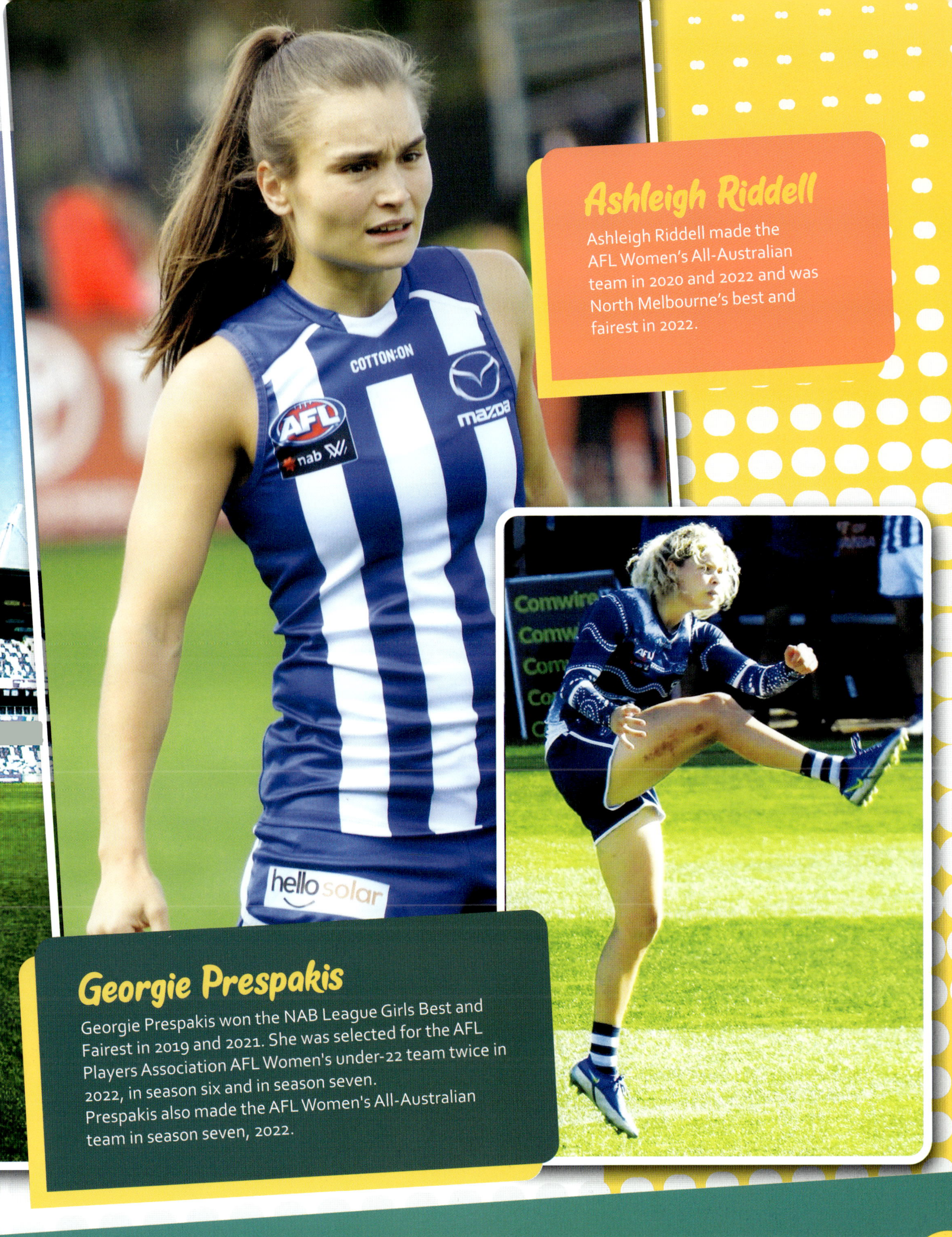

Ashleigh Riddell

Ashleigh Riddell made the AFL Women's All-Australian team in 2020 and 2022 and was North Melbourne's best and fairest in 2022.

Georgie Prespakis

Georgie Prespakis won the NAB League Girls Best and Fairest in 2019 and 2021. She was selected for the AFL Players Association AFL Women's under-22 team twice in 2022, in season six and in season seven. Prespakis also made the AFL Women's All-Australian team in season seven, 2022.

Maddy Prespakis

Prespakis won the 2019 AFL Women's Rising Star award and the 2020 AFL Women's best and fairest award. She is a three-time AFL Women's All-Australian, three-time Carlton best and fairest winner and was the inaugural Essendon best and fairest winner in season seven.

Kiara Bowers

Kiara Bowers made her debut a the four point win against Melbourne in the opening round of the 2019 season. She was voted as the Most Valuable player in her second season and was named in the 2019 AFL Women's All-Australian team. In 2020, she won the best player award in the first ever AFL Women's Western Derby and was again named in the All-Australian team.

Erin Phillips

Erin Phillips is a two-time WNBA champion and Olympic basketballer who successfully transitioned to football. In the inaugural season, she won the AFLW Best and Fairest, AFL Players Association MVP and the Crows Club Champion award.

Brianna Davey

Brianna Davey won the inaugural Carlton best and fairest award and was named in the 2017 AFL Women's All-Australian team. She served as Carlton captain from 2018 to 2019 before being appointed Collingwood co-captain in 2021. She also won the league best and fairest award for the 2021 season.

THE AFLW TEAMS

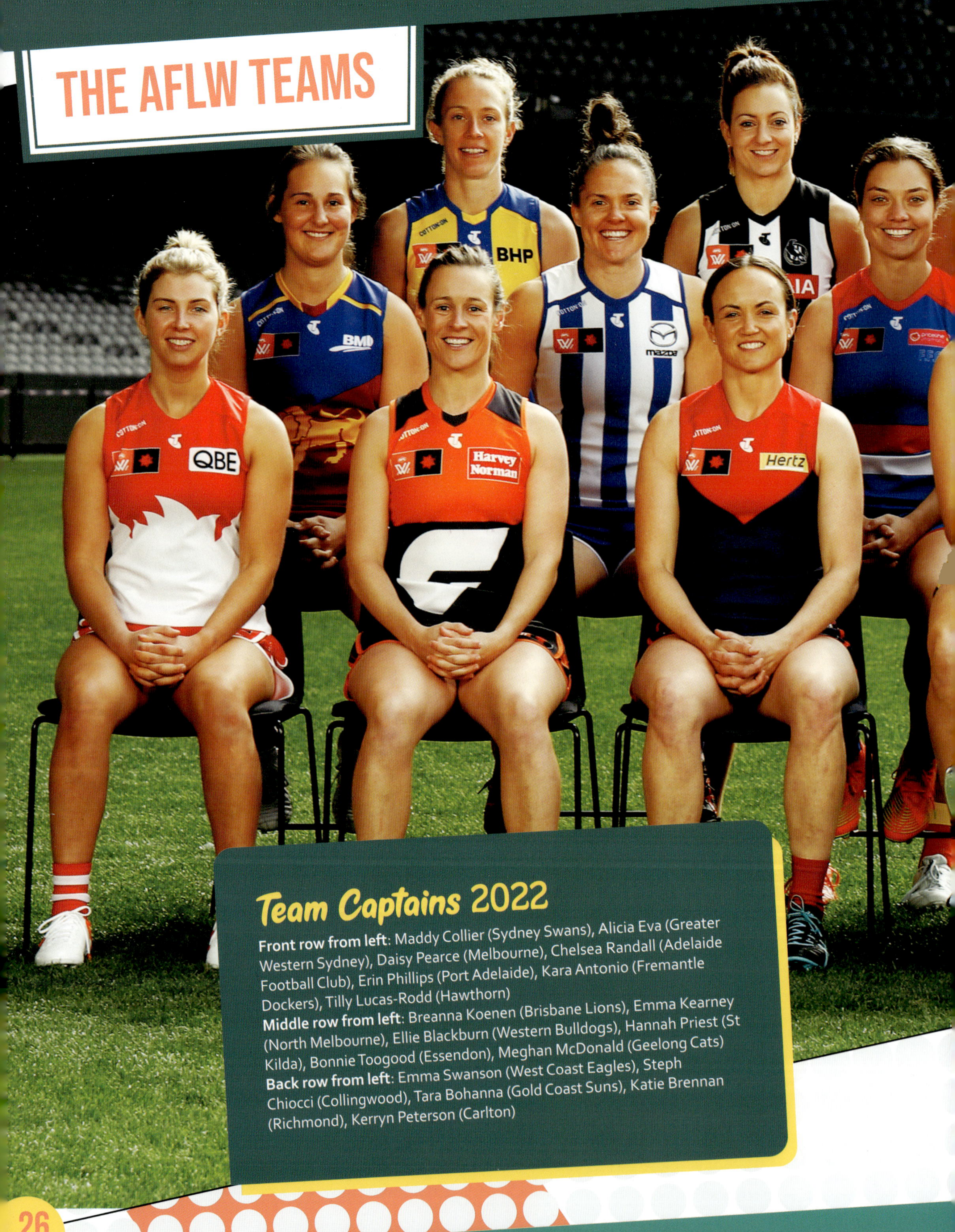

Team Captains 2022

Front row from left: Maddy Collier (Sydney Swans), Alicia Eva (Greater Western Sydney), Daisy Pearce (Melbourne), Chelsea Randall (Adelaide Football Club), Erin Phillips (Port Adelaide), Kara Antonio (Fremantle Dockers), Tilly Lucas-Rodd (Hawthorn)
Middle row from left: Breanna Koenen (Brisbane Lions), Emma Kearney (North Melbourne), Ellie Blackburn (Western Bulldogs), Hannah Priest (St Kilda), Bonnie Toogood (Essendon), Meghan McDonald (Geelong Cats)
Back row from left: Emma Swanson (West Coast Eagles), Steph Chiocci (Collingwood), Tara Bohanna (Gold Coast Suns), Katie Brennan (Richmond), Kerryn Peterson (Carlton)

WEST COAST EAGLES
WESTCOASTEAGLES.COM.AU
The Eagles
COLLINGWOOD
COLLINGWOODFC.COM.AU
The Pies
GOLD COAST SUNS
GOLDCOASTFC.COM.AU
The Suns
RICHMOND
RICHMONDFC.COM.AU
The Tigers
CARLTON
CARLTONFC.COM.AU
The Baggers
BRISBANE LIONS
LIONS.COM.AU
The Lions
NORTH MELBOURNE
NMFC.COM.AU
The Roos
WESTERN BULLDOGS
WESTERNBULLDOGS.COM.AU
The Bulldogs
ST KILDA
SAINTS.COM.AU
The Saints
ESSENDON
ESSENDONFC.COM.AU
The Bombers
GEELONG CATS
GEELONGCATS.COM.AU
The Cats
SYDNEY SWANS
SYDNEYSWANS.COM.AU
The Swans
GREATER WESTERN SYDNEY GIANTS
GWSGIANTS.COM.AU
The Giants
MELBOURNE
MELBOURNEFC.COM.AU
The Demons
ADELAIDE
AFC.COM.AU
The Crows
PORT ADELAIDE
PORTADELAIDEFC.COM.AU
The Power
FREMANTLE DOCKERS
FREMANTLEFC.COM.AU
The Dockers
HAWTHORNE
HAWTHORNFC.COM.AU
The Hawks

THE MVP AWARD

The AFLW Players' Most Valuable Player award is voted on by the players' peers and was first presented in 2017 .

Erin Phillips

2017

AFL Women's premiership
AFL Women's Grand Final best-on-ground
AFLW Players' most valuable player
AFL Women's All-Australian team
AFL Women's Goal of the Year
Adelaide Crows Club Champion

2019

AFL Women's premiership
AFL Women's Grand Final best-on-ground
AFLW Players' most valuable player
AFLW Coaches' champion player of the year
AFL Women's All-Australian team
Adelaide Crows Club Champion

Emma Kearney

2018

AFL Women's premiership
AFL Women's All-Australian team
Western Bulldogs best and fairest

Kiara Bowers

2021

AFLW Coaches' champion player of the year
AFL Women's All-Australian team
Fremantle Dockers best and fairest

Madison Prespakis

2020

AFL Women's All-Australian team
Carlton best and fairest
AFL Women's 22under22 team

Brianna Davey

2021

AFLW Players' most valuable player
AFL Women's All-Australian team
Collingwood best and fairest

Emily Bates

2022

AFLW Players' most valuable player
AFLW Coaches' champion player of the year
AFL Women's All-Australian team
Brisbane best and fairest

AFLW PREMIERSHIP WINNERS

2017

ADELAIDE CROWS 4.11 (35) defeated BRISBANE 4.5 (29), at Metricon Stadium

2018

WESTERN BULLDOGS 4.3 (27) defeated BRISBANE 3.3 (21), at Ikon Park

2019

ADELAIDE CROWS 10.3 (63) defeated CARLTON 2.6 (18), at Adelaide Oval

2020

Cancelled due to Covid-19 restrictions

2021

BRISBANE 6.2 (38) defeated ADELAIDE CROWS 3.2 (20) at Adelaide Oval

2022

MELBOURNE DEMONS 2.7 (19)defeated BRISBANE 2.3 (15) at Brighton Homes Arena

GLOSSARY

bench interchange area where players wait to take over from exhausted players

bustle move the ball without taking possession of it

disposal passing the ball legally, via a handball or kick

flank ground that lies between the wing and pocket on both sides of the centre

goal square rectangle in front of the goal posts from which the ball is kicked after scoring a behind

Grand Final final game of the season in which the premiership is decided

on the full kicked ball that hasn't bounced or been touched by any player

out-of-bounds ball or player who has crossed the boundary line of the field of play

overhead marking catching the ball with hands extended above the head

packs large group of players around the ball

possession when a player grabs the ball and takes control of it

professional a sportsperson who accepts payment for playing a sport

stoppages when play stops for a ball up or a throw in

tactics a game plan developed by a coach to gain an advantage over the opposition

INDEX

Adelaide Crows 6, 8, 24, 25, 27, 28, 30
Brisbane Lions 6, 26, 30
Carlton 6, 19, 24-26, 29, 30
centre line 7
Collingwood 6, 19, 25, 26, 29
Daisy Pearce 20
draft 6
Essendon 24, 27
forward line 7
free kick 11, 12, 15
Fremantle Dockers 8, 21, 22, 24, 26, 28
full-back 7
full-forward 7
Geelong 20, 23, 27
half-back line 7
half-forward line 7
Melbourne Demons 4, 20, 26
North Melbourne 23, 27
Port Adelaide 25, 27
Richmond 27
ruck 7, 11, 12
St Kilda 8, 27
Sydney Swans 27
Tayla Harris 4, 20, 21
training 8, 9
umpires 10, 11, 13-15
West Coast Eagles 27
Western Australia 18, 20, 23
Western Bulldogs 22, 26, 28, 30